Tongues and Tails

HEAD TO TAIL
TONGUES
· AND ·
TAILS

WRITTEN BY
THERESA GREENAWAY

SCIENTIFIC CONSULTANT JOYCE POPE
ILLUSTRATED BY ANN SAVAGE,
JULIAN AND JANET BAKER

RSVP
RAINTREE
Steck-Vaughn
PUBLISHERS
The Steck-Vaughn Company

Austin, Texas

© **Copyright this edition 1995 Steck-Vaughn Company**

All rights reserved. No part of the material protected by this copyright may be reproduced or utilized in any form or by any means, electronic or mechanical, including photocopying, recording, or by any information storage and retrieval system, without permission in writing from the copyright owner. Requests for permission to make copies of any part of the work should be mailed to: Copyright Permissions, Steck-Vaughn Company, P.O. Box 26015, Austin, TX 78755

Library of Congress Cataloging-in-Publication Data

Greenaway, Theresa, 1947–
Tongues and tails / by Theresa Greenaway;
illustrated by Ann Savage and Julian and Janet Baker.
p. cm. — (Head to tail)
Includes index.
ISBN 0-8114-8271-5
1. Tongue—Juvenile literature. 2. Tail—Juvenile literature.
3. Animals—Juvenile literature. [1. Tongue. 2. Tail. 3. Animals.]
I. Savage, Ann, 1951– ill. II. Baker, Julian, 1956– ill.
III. Baker, Janet, 1957– ill. IV. Title. V. Series.
QL946.G74   1995
591.1'82—dc20
94-16739   CIP   AC

Editors: Wendy Madgwick and Kim Merlino
Designer: Janie Louise Hunt

Printed in Spain
1 2 3 4 5 6 7 8 9 0 LB 99 98 97 96 95 94

Contents

All About Tongues ...6
All About Tails ...8
A Quick Snack ...10
Hold on Tight ...12
Lapping It Up ...14
A Stinger in the Tail ...16
A Tiny Feast! ...18
Sending Messages ...20
On the Move ...22
Go Away! ...24
Special Tails ...26
Is It Tasty? ...28
Mother Care ...30
What a Tail! ...32
Quiz ...34
Glossary ...36
Index ...38

All About Tongues

Look at your tongue in a mirror. See how it moves. Feel its rough surface. Tongues help you taste food. Taste is important. It keeps an animal from eating things that can make it sick. Tiny taste buds are on the tongue. They tell you if something is sweet, sour, bitter, or salty. Some animals have tongues that can do much more than this. They can catch insects, suck up nectar, or lick a cub. Some tongues can frighten away an enemy!

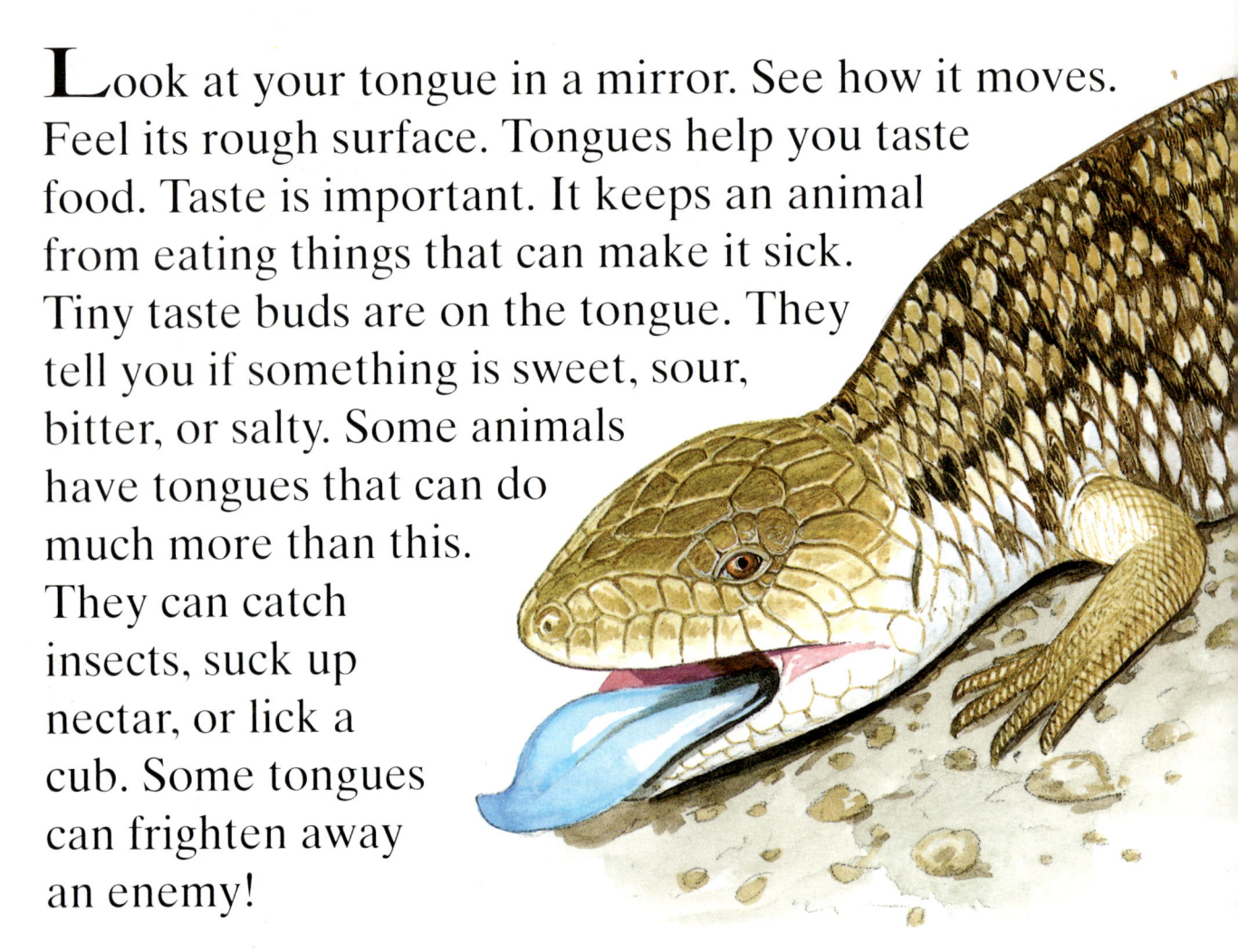

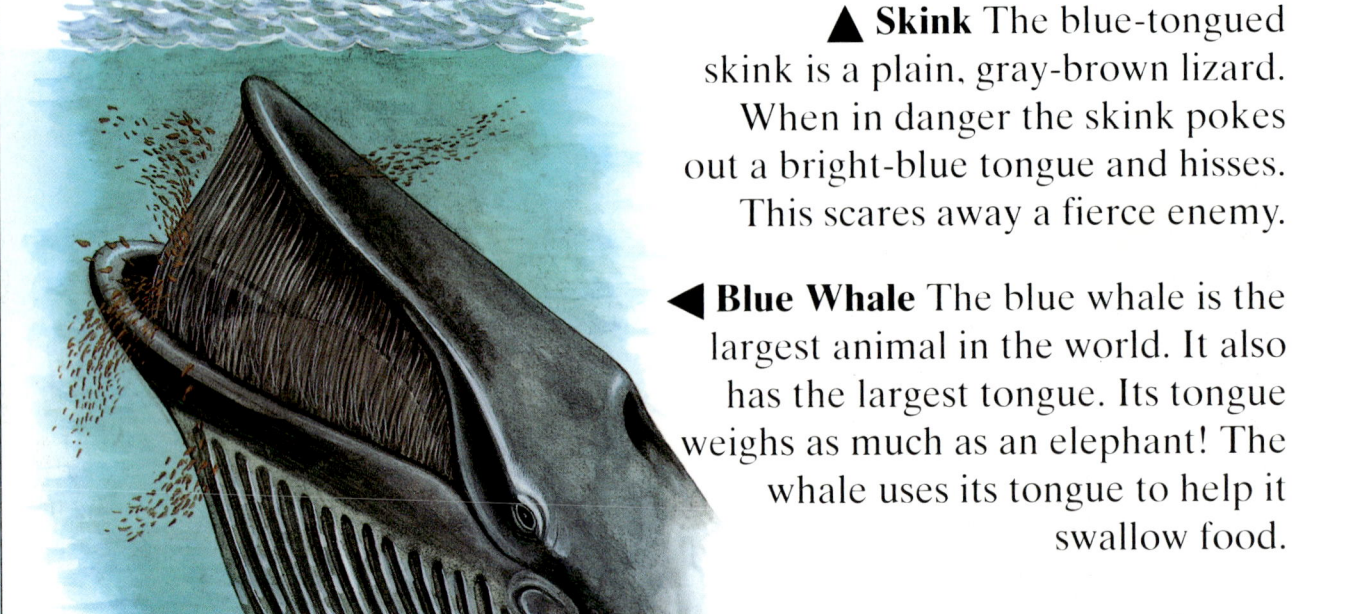

▲ **Skink** The blue-tongued skink is a plain, gray-brown lizard. When in danger the skink pokes out a bright-blue tongue and hisses. This scares away a fierce enemy.

◀ **Blue Whale** The blue whale is the largest animal in the world. It also has the largest tongue. Its tongue weighs as much as an elephant! The whale uses its tongue to help it swallow food.

▶ **Penguins** These macaroni penguins eat fish. They catch the fish under the water and swallow them whole. A penguin's tongue and the roof of its mouth have spines that point backward. The spines help the penguin hold on to the fish.

▼ **Gaur** This large gaur is a wild bull from India. It uses its tongue to eat grass. The gaur wraps its tongue around a large clump of grass. Then it pulls the grass into its mouth.

▼ **Snakes** A snake uses its tongue to "taste" the air. Its tongue picks up any smells in the air. These smells tell the snake if any animals are close by.

All About Tails

Most birds and animals with four legs have a tail. Tails come in all shapes and sizes. Some tails are furry, and some are scaly. Others are mostly feathers. Tails can be moved. They can be waved backward and forward. They can help the animal move. Tails can even be wrapped around an animal to keep it warm.

▲ **Shingleback Skink** Which end of this lizard is its head? The lizard has a short fat tail that looks just like a head. Then an enemy comes near. The shingleback moves its tail as if it were its head. The enemy tries to catch it. But the lizard runs away in the other direction!

▼ **Rats** The bushytail wood rat's tail is long and furry. The brown rat has a scaly tail with no fur.

bushytail wood rat

brown rat

▼ **Trout** Fish like this rainbow trout move their tails from side to side. This is how they swim through the water.

▲ **Swallow** The swallow flies with twists and turns. Its long, forked tail helps it fly this way. The swallow opens and closes its tail to move with grace. It catches insects in flight, too.

▲ **Bombardier Beetle** This little beetle attacks an enemy that comes too close. It squirts out a fluid from its tail. The fluid explodes in its attacker's face.

A Quick Snack

Some animals feed on other animals. An animal does not wish to be caught by its enemy. It must move quickly. But some hunters have found a way to catch these fast-moving animals. They have a long, sticky tongue. They can flick it out to catch their meal. Other animals have even better ways.

▼ **Toad** The toad hides among leaves and plants on the ground. A creepy crawly moves past. The toad flicks out its tongue and catches it.

▼ **Frog** When a frog sees a fly on a nearby leaf, it leaps to catch it. At the same time, it flicks out its sticky tongue. Only the fastest flies escape.

▲ **Chameleon** The chameleon sits very still on a leafy twig. When a fly lands nearby, the lizard flicks out its tongue. The fly sticks to the tip of the tongue. Then the lizard pulls its tongue, and the fly, back into its mouth.

▼ **Snapping Turtle** The alligator snapping turtle lies on the bottom of the water. Its mouth is open. On its tongue is a red wormlike thing that the turtle wiggles. When a little fish swims up to look at the worm — snap! The turtle eats the fish.

▲ **Archerfish** An archerfish spots a fly on a leaf. It stops swimming. It takes careful aim and then shoots a jet of water. The water knocks the fly off the leaf into the fish's mouth!

Hold on Tight

Some animals live in trees or under the water. Here, plants and seaweeds are often moved by wind or waves. The animals here must have a firm hold on the plants. If they do not, they may be swept away. Or they may fall when they move. Many animals use their tails to hold on to things. This leaves their hands and feet free to do other jobs.

▼ **Spider Monkey** The black spider monkey lives in the Amazon rain forest. Its tail is very strong. The monkey hangs by its tail. Then it can reach down and pick fruit from branches far below it.

▲ **Spotted Cuscus** The cuscus feeds at night. It climbs through the treetops looking for food. As it climbs, the cuscus wraps its tail around the wet branches. This way it does not slip. There is a bare patch of skin on the tip of its tail. This gives it an even better grip.

▲ **Silky Anteater** This little anteater is often hunted by the harpy eagle. Sometimes an eagle flies too close. The anteater holds on by its tail. It can then strike out. It uses its paws, which have long claws.

▼ **Harvest Mouse** Tiny harvest mice climb up and down tall stems of grass. They even build their small, round nests among the stems. The grass often moves in the wind. To keep from falling, the mice coil their tails around the grass stems.

▼ **Sea Horse** This strange little fish lives close to the shore. When the waves are rough, the sea horse coils its tail around the seaweed. Then it is not washed away.

Lapping It Up

Some animals feed on the sweet nectar made by flowers. Many of these animals have long tongues. They use them to reach deep into the flower. Then they suck, or lap up, the nectar. Some animals also feed on pollen from flowers.

◀ **Monarch Butterfly**
Butterflies have very long tongues. Their tongues are something like straws. The butterfly pokes its tongue deep into the flower. Then it sucks up the nectar. When it has finished, it coils its tongue up again.

▼ **Sunbird** The malachite sunbird feeds on nectar from brightly colored flowers. It has a forked tongue. It presses the top fork of its tongue against its beak. This forms a tube. Then it sucks the nectar out of the flowers.

▲ **Vampire Bat**
The vampire bat feeds on blood. It makes a cut in the animal's skin. It then laps up the blood with its grooved tongue.

▼ **Long-Nosed Bat** This tiny bat lives in tropical Central America. It has a long tongue with a brushlike tip. It laps up the nectar from the flowers and also collects the pollen.

▼ **Housefly** A fly has a spongelike tip to its tongue. It uses its tongue to suck up liquid from all sorts of food, including your dinner!

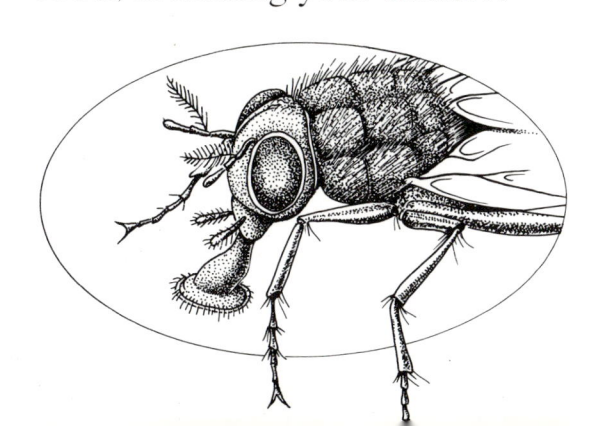

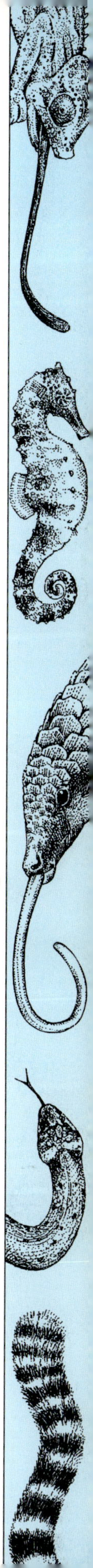

A Stinger in the Tail

A tail can also be used as a weapon. Long tails that bend can be used to hit an enemy. Some animals have a stinger in their tails. They use it to inject poison into another animal. The poison kills the animal or keeps it from moving.

▲ **Scorpions** Scorpions are fierce hunters. They have a poisonous stinger in their tail. They use it to keep large prey from moving. Often an enemy comes too close. Then the scorpion lifts up its tail and stings its enemy. Some scorpions' poison is strong enough to kill a person!

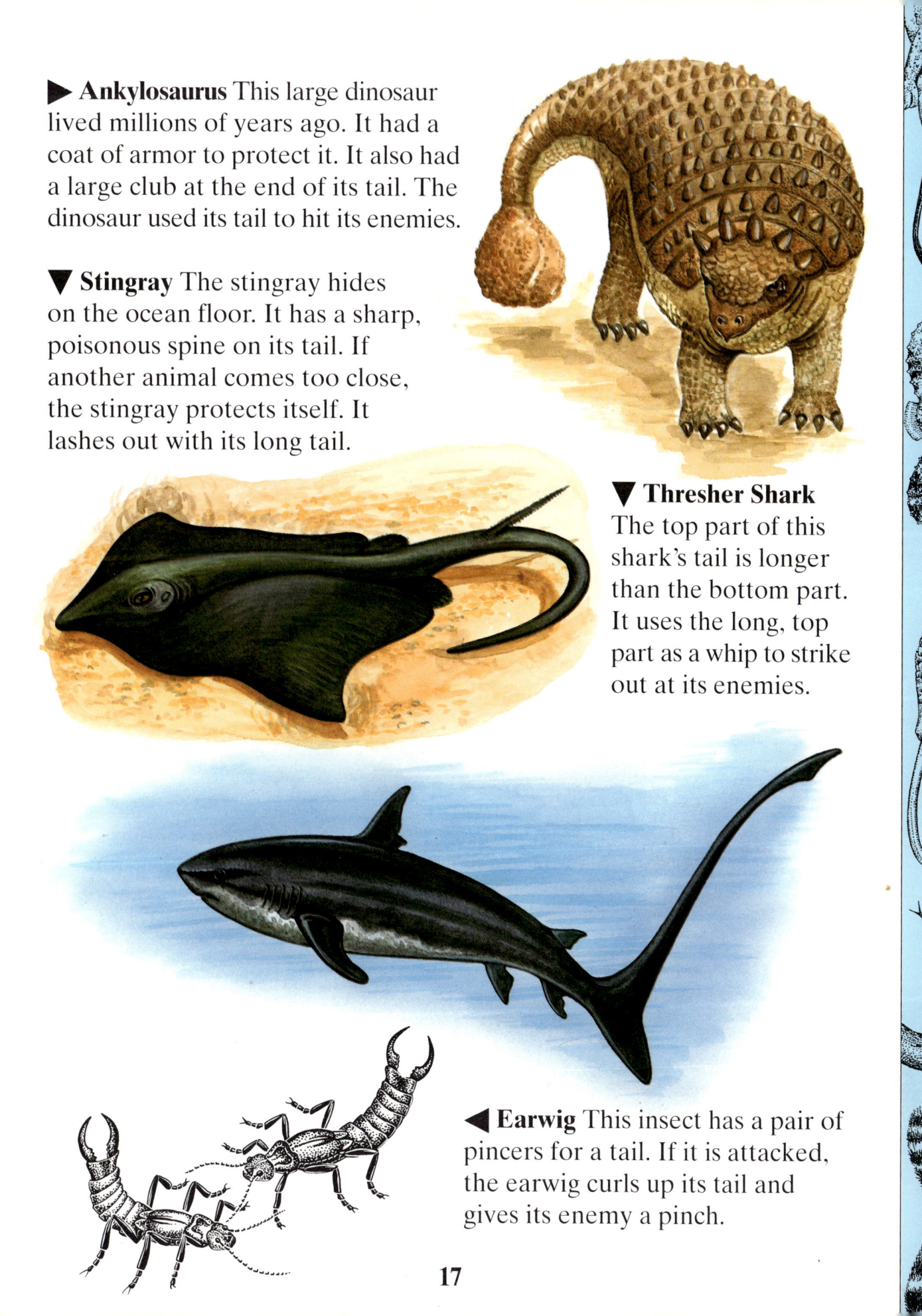

▶ **Ankylosaurus** This large dinosaur lived millions of years ago. It had a coat of armor to protect it. It also had a large club at the end of its tail. The dinosaur used its tail to hit its enemies.

▼ **Stingray** The stingray hides on the ocean floor. It has a sharp, poisonous spine on its tail. If another animal comes too close, the stingray protects itself. It lashes out with its long tail.

▼ **Thresher Shark** The top part of this shark's tail is longer than the bottom part. It uses the long, top part as a whip to strike out at its enemies.

◀ **Earwig** This insect has a pair of pincers for a tail. If it is attacked, the earwig curls up its tail and gives its enemy a pinch.

A Tiny Feast!

Many birds and animals feed on tiny ants and termites. But ants and termites are fierce little animals. They have strong jaws to bite their enemies. They also spray stinging liquids that will drive their enemy away. Animals that eat them have special ways of collecting their meal.

▼ **Aardvark** Aardvarks hunt at night. They break open a termite mound with their claws. The termites run out. Then the aardvark licks them up with its long, sticky tongue.

▶ **Giant Pangolin** The giant pangolin has one of the longest tongues — 28 inches (71 cm) long. It can eat up to 200,000 ants in one night!

◀ **Giant Anteater** The giant anteater has a long, pointed nose and a tiny mouth. But inside its mouth it has a sticky, 2-foot-long (60 cm) tongue! It can flick its tongue in and out 150 times a minute. This way it picks up hundreds of ants each time.

▼ **Short-beaked Echidna** This echidna flicks out its thin, sticky tongue. That is how it picks up fat ants and termites.

▲ **Green Woodpecker** The green woodpecker drills a hole into an ants' nest. It then pushes its tongue into the hole. The ants get glued to its sticky tip.

19

Sending Messages

An animal's tail can tell you how it is feeling. A cat lashes its tail from side to side when it is angry. If a dog is frightened, it tucks its tail between its legs. Other animals hold their tails up to greet a friend or warn of danger. Tails can be used to give many different messages.

▲ **Beaver** The beaver has a flat, scaly tail. When it is in danger, it slaps the water with its tail. The loud noise this makes warns the other beavers, so they can escape.

◀ **Crested Newt** The male newt grows a large red crest along his back and tail. This crest forms in the spring. It helps him attract a female mate.

▶ **Spotted Skunks** An enemy might come too close. The spotted skunk bangs its feet and raises its black-and-white tail to warn the enemy off. If this does not work, the skunk does a handstand. Then it sprays its enemy with a foul-smelling liquid.

◀ **Whitetail Deer** If a whitetail deer sees danger, it puts its tail straight up. This shows its white tail patch and warns other deer of the danger.

▼ **Dog** When a dog is pleased, it wags its tail. If it is frightened, it puts its tail between its legs!

On the Move

A tail can be used to help an animal move around. It can help an animal swing through the trees or swim in the water. It even helps them glide through the air. Many animals' tails are specially shaped to help them move.

▶ **Red Kangaroo** Kangaroos live in the bush in Australia. They hop around on their large back legs. Their long, heavy tail helps them balance so that they do not fall over.

◀ **Feathertail Glider** This little pouched animal from Australia lives in the trees. It glides from one tree to another. It uses its fluffy tail to help it go in the right direction.

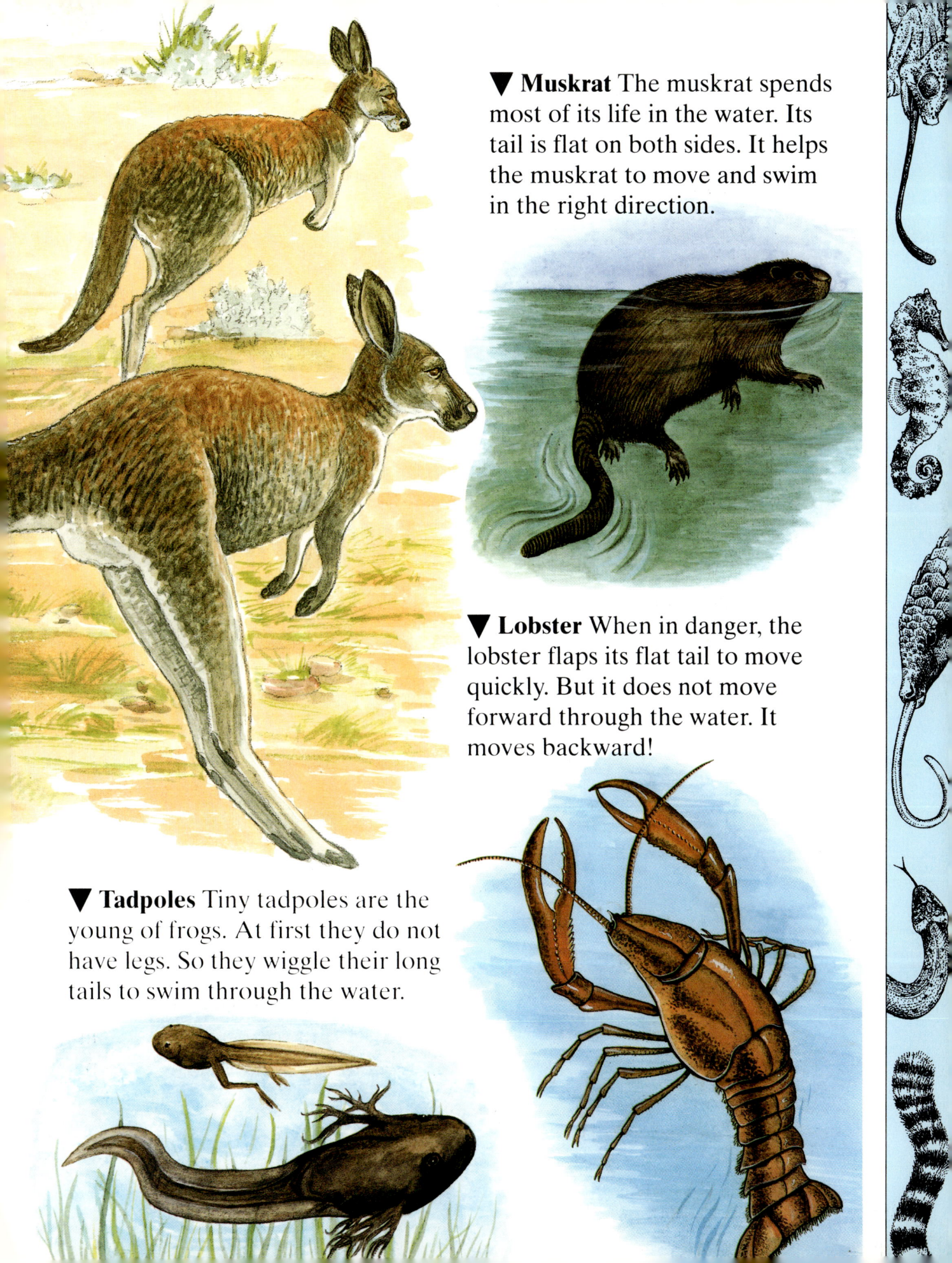

▼ **Muskrat** The muskrat spends most of its life in the water. Its tail is flat on both sides. It helps the muskrat to move and swim in the right direction.

▼ **Lobster** When in danger, the lobster flaps its flat tail to move quickly. But it does not move forward through the water. It moves backward!

▼ **Tadpoles** Tiny tadpoles are the young of frogs. At first they do not have legs. So they wiggle their long tails to swim through the water.

Go Away!

Some animals scare away an enemy by giving it a shock! An animal shows a flash of color or makes a loud noise. Or it moves suddenly. All these actions help give the animal time to escape.

▼ **Puss Moth Caterpillar**
A bird or insect that attacks the puss moth caterpillar is in for a shock. The caterpillar rears up to show its bright face. It also lashes out with the red threads at the end of its tail.

▼ **Lizard** Many lizards have a special way to escape. If a lizard's enemy catches its tail, it simply lets its tail drop off! It will soon grow a new tail.

◀ **Leaf-tailed Gecko**
The leaf-tailed gecko lives in Madagascar. It hunts at night. In daytime, it sits on tree trunks. Its color matches the tree trunk, so it is hard to see. But if an enemy comes too close, the gecko moves fast. It opens its mouth wide to show its red tongue and flaps its tail. Its fierce looks scare away the enemy.

▲ **Rattlesnake** If something comes too close to a rattlesnake, it makes a warning sound. It rattles the loose scales on its tail. This tells other animals to beware.

◀ **Spectacled Salamander**
This gray salamander hides beside streams in the day. If a bird tries to catch it, the salamander has a special trick. It flips its tail up and over to show the red underside. It also stays very still!

Special Tails

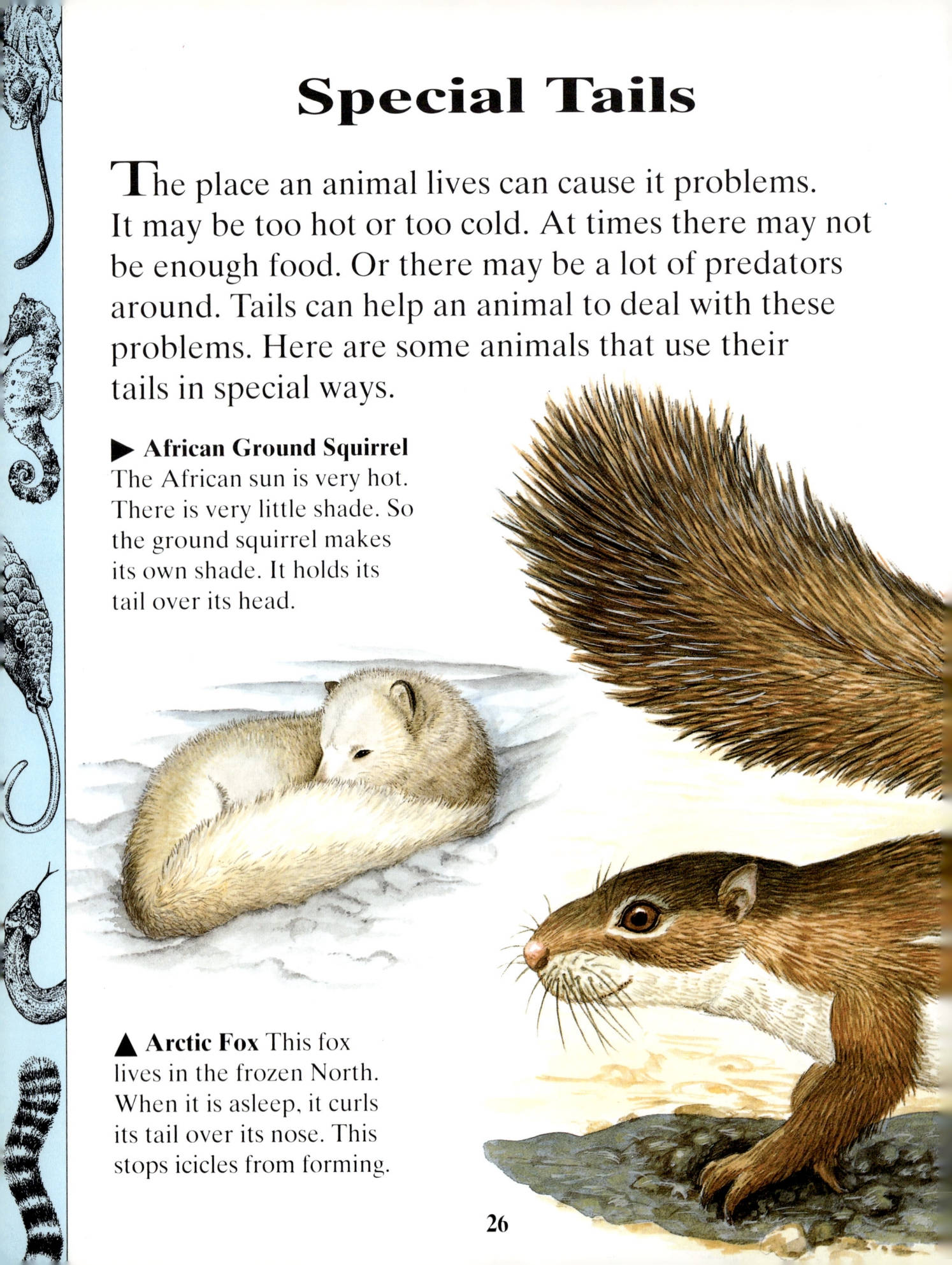

The place an animal lives can cause it problems. It may be too hot or too cold. At times there may not be enough food. Or there may be a lot of predators around. Tails can help an animal to deal with these problems. Here are some animals that use their tails in special ways.

▶ **African Ground Squirrel** The African sun is very hot. There is very little shade. So the ground squirrel makes its own shade. It holds its tail over its head.

▲ **Arctic Fox** This fox lives in the frozen North. When it is asleep, it curls its tail over its nose. This stops icicles from forming.

▼ **Fat-tailed Dunnart** This is a little, pouched animal. It eats all the time when there is a lot of food around. Its tail gets fatter and fatter! When there is little food to eat, it goes to sleep and lives off its fat.

▼ **Horse** Horses have long tails. When it's hot, a horse flicks its tail up and down. This helps to keep flies from landing on the horse's body and biting it.

▼ **Garden Eel** These eels have very hard tips on their tails. They use them to dig into the ocean floor. Each eel lives safe and sound inside its burrow. It only sticks its head out to eat.

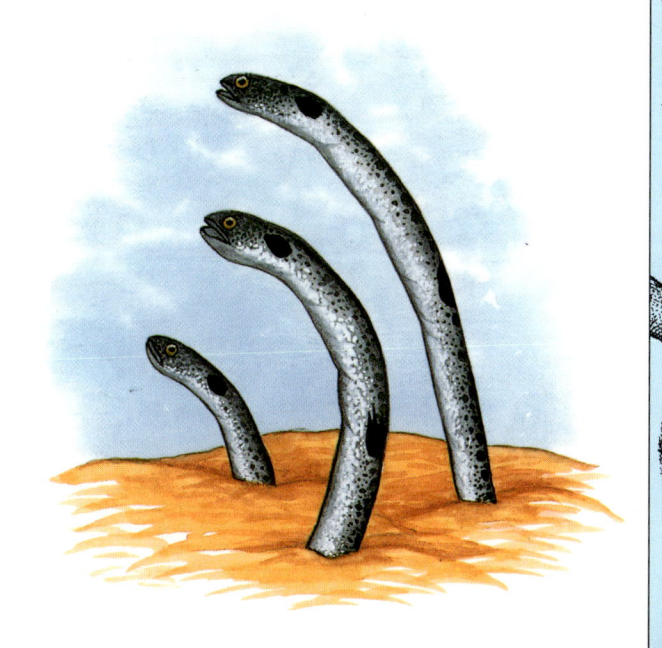

Is It Tasty?

If you are not sure about a new food, you might sniff it first. So do animals. They sniff and lick their food to make sure it's safe. Some plant and animal food tastes awful. It can make the eater sick. Animals soon learn not to eat those foods.

▲ **Macaw**
A macaw eats fruits and nuts. It holds its food in its claws and tastes it with its tongue. It also uses its tongue to move food around in its beak.

▼ **Koala** The koala lives in Australia. It is a very fussy eater. There are six hundred kinds of eucalyptus trees in Australia. The koala only likes the taste of seventeen of them.

▼ **Langur** The hanuman langur feeds on fruit. If the fruit is unripe and tastes sour, the langur will throw it away. It only likes ripe, sweet fruit.

▶ **Red-Fronted Lemur** Lemurs eat giant millipedes. Millipedes move slowly and are very easy to catch. But they have a foul-tasting poison on them. Before the lemur eats a millipede, it rubs off the poison with its tail. Then it eats it up!

Mother Care

Many female animals care for their babies. A mother cat will lick her kittens to keep them clean. Other animals will wrap their tails around their young. This way they keep them warm. This loving care helps the mother and her baby to know each other.

▼ **Skink** Lizards do not often care for their young. The Great Plains skink does. She guards her eggs and licks the babies clean when they hatch.

▼ **Sheep** When a mother sheep gives birth to a lamb, she licks it clean. This helps the tiny lamb know its mother.

◀ **Tiger** The tiger belongs to the cat family. The mother tiger licks her cubs with her rough tongue. This keeps them clean.

▼ **Brown-Tail Moth** The hairs on the tail of this moth can hurt other animals. The female puts some hairs on her eggs. This keeps other insects from eating them.

◀ **Noctule** This bat hangs upside down by its feet when it rests. When the female is about to give birth, she turns the right way up. This means she can catch her tiny baby in her tail flap.

What a Tail!

Some tails are useful. Some are beautiful. Some are both! Animals spend a lot of time looking after their tails. Here are a few of the biggest and best tails.

▶ **Superb Lyrebird** When a male superb lyrebird sees a female, he opens up his tail. The bright silvery feathers shine in the sun. This way the female can't miss him.

▼ **Blue Tang** This bright little fish lives on the Great Barrier Reef. Its body is striped blue. It has a bright yellow tail.

▶ **Giant Anteater** The giant anteater's tail is like a thick blanket. It helps to keep it warm at night.

▼ **Ring-tailed Lemur** The lemur has a splendid black-and-white striped tail. It is over 20 inches (50 cm) long. It is both beautiful and useful! A male lemur sometimes fights. It uses its smelly tail and loud voice to scare its enemies.

Quiz

1. How does a snake "taste" the air?

2. How do harvest mice keep from falling when they climb?

3. Why does the monarch butterfly have a long tongue?

4. Which animals do these tongues belong to?

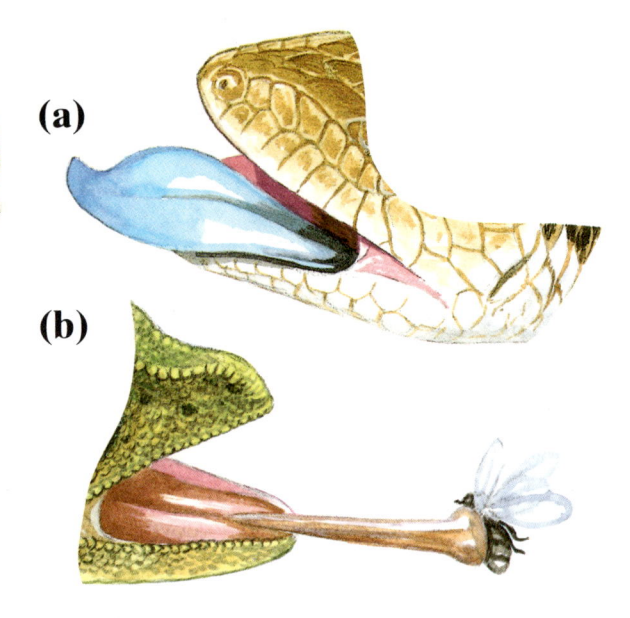

(a)

(b)

5. How does this Australian animal move?

34

6. How does the beaver warn other beavers of danger?

7. Which animals do these tails belong to?

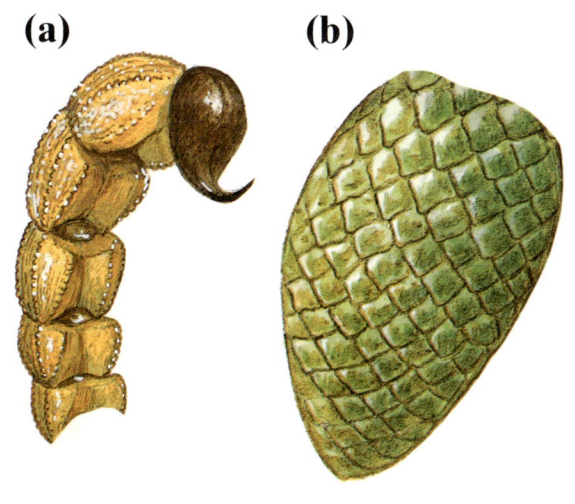

(a)   (b)

8. What is a sea horse?

9. How can you tell if a dog is pleased?

10. How did Ankylosaurus use its tail?

11. How much does a blue whale's tongue weigh?

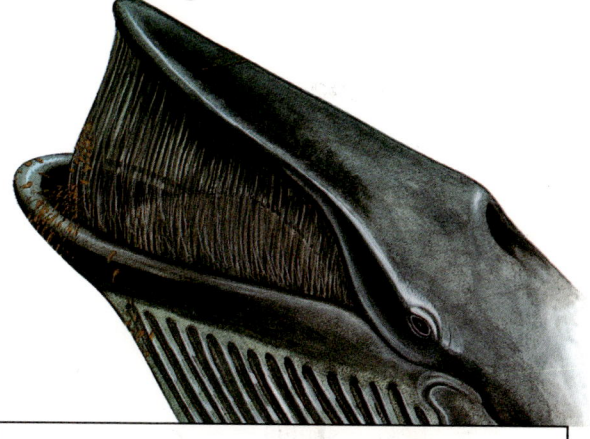

If you do not know the answers turn to the following pages:
1. p7, **2.** p13, **3.** p14, **4a.** p7, **4b.** p11, **5.** p22, **6.** p20, **7a.** p16, **7b.** p8, **8.** p13, **9.** p21, **10.** p17, **11.** p6

Glossary

Bull The male of several cattlelike animals.

Burrow A large tunnel that many kinds of animals dig in the ground. Sometimes the animals live in their burrows. Sometimes they dig them to find food.

Caterpillar A name for a stage in the life of a butterfly or moth. The caterpillar hatches from an egg. (See **Eggs** and **Hatch**.)

Claw A long, sharp nail on an animal's foot. Also the pincers of animals such as crabs and scorpions.

Coil To wrap around and around an object.

Crest A frill of skin that some animals have on their heads or backs.

Cub The young of animals such as the lion and bear.

Dinosaur A kind of reptile that lived millions of years ago. None are alive today. (See **Reptile**.)

Eggs Small, round objects laid by a female. Young animals hatch from eggs. Birds, reptiles, and many insects lay eggs. (See **Reptile** and **Insect**.)

Forked Something that splits into two at its tip.

Frog An animal that lives on land and in water. A frog has a small body with smooth, wet skin. It has small front legs and very large back legs. An adult frog has no tail.

Great Barrier Reef A large strip of rocks made by tiny coral animals. It lies beneath the sea off Australia.

Hatch When a baby animal breaks out of its egg. (See **Eggs**.)

Hunter An animal that kills and eats other animals. (See **Predator**.)

Inject To squirt a liquid into something.

Insect A small animal with six legs. The adult has a hard case around its body. Most insects have two or four wings.

Lizard A lizard is an animal with scaly skin. Most lizards have four legs. They belong to a group of animals called reptiles.

Millipede A long, worm-shaped animal with lots of legs.

Nectar A sweet, sugary liquid made by flowers. Many small animals feed on nectar.

Nest A special place made and lived in by an animal. Some animals lay their eggs or bring up their young in a nest.

Poison A substance that can harm an animal.

Pollen The yellow powder made in the male parts of a flower. Bees, bats, beetles, and other small animals eat pollen.

Pouched animal An animal that cares for its young in a pocket or pouch. These animals are called marsupials.

Predator An animal that kills and eats another animal. (See **Hunter**.)

Reptile An animal with scaly skin. Most reptiles lay eggs. Lizards, snakes, and turtles are reptiles.

Scales Thick, hard skin with no hair on it. A snake's and lizard's skin is covered with scales. These scales are made of a hard material like your fingernails.

Snake A scaly animal that does not have any legs. It moves by wiggling over the ground. Snakes belong to the group of animals called reptiles.

Spine A hard, pointed part on an animal's body.

Stinger A sharp needlelike part of an animal's body that can inject poison.

Tadpole The young stage of a frog or toad. It has a head and a tail but no legs. The legs grow later as the tadpole gets bigger.

Taste bud A special spot on the tongue that helps you taste food. Taste buds help you tell if something is sweet, sour, salty, or bitter.

Termite mound The nest of a group of termites. These insects make tall homes from mud and saliva (spit). This bakes hard in the hot sun to make a strong nest.

Toad A small animal with a short, fat body and rough, dry skin. It has small front legs and large back legs. The toad is related to the frog. (See **Frog**.)

Turtle An animal with a scaly skin and a shell. Turtles belong to a group of animals called reptiles.

Index

A
Aardvark 18
African ground squirrel 26
Alligator snapping turtle 11
Amazon rain forest 12
Ankylosaurus 17
Ants 18, 19
Archerfish 11
Arctic fox 26

B
Bats 15, 31
Beaver 20
Blue tang 32
Blue whale 6
Bombardier beetle 9
Brown rat 9
Brown-tail moth 31
Bushytail wood rat 9
Butterflies 14

C
Chameleon 11
Crested newt 21

D
Dinosaur 17
Dog 21

E
Earwig 17

F
Fat-tailed dunnart 27
Feathertail glider 22
Frog 10

G
Garden eel 27
Gaur 7
Giant anteater 19, 33
Giant pangolin 18
Great Barrier Reef 32
Great Plains skink 30
Green woodpecker 19

H
Hanuman langur 29
Harvest mouse 13
Horse 27
Housefly 15
Hunters 10

I
Insects 6, 9

K
Koala 29

L
Langur 29
Leaf-tailed gecko 25
Lizard 24, 30
Lobster 23
Long-nosed bat 15

M
Macaw 28
Malachite sunbird 15
Millipedes 29
Monarch butterfly 14
Muskrat 23

N
Noctule (bat) 31
Nectar 6, 14, 15

P
Penguins 7
Pollen 14, 15
Puss moth caterpillar 24

R
Rainbow trout 9
Rats 9
Rattlesnake 25
Red-fronted lemur 29
Red kangaroo 22
Ring-tailed lemur 33

S
Salamander 25
Scorpion 16
Sea horse 13
Sheep 30
Shingleback skink 8
Short-beaked echidna 19
Silky anteater 13
Skink 6, 30
Snakes 7, 25
Snapping turtle 11
Spectacled salamander 25
Spider monkey 12
Spotted cuscus 12
Spotted skunk 21
Stinger 16
Stingray 17
Sunbird 15
Superb lyrebird 32
Swallow 9

T
Tadpoles 23
Tails 8, 9, 12, 13, 16, 17, 20, 21, 22, 23, 24, 25, 26, 27, 29, 30, 31, 32, 33
Taste 6
Taste buds 6
Termite mound 18
Termites 18, 19
Thresher shark 17
Tiger 31
Toad 10
Tongues 6, 7, 10, 11, 14, 15, 18, 19, 25, 28, 30, 31
Trout 9

V
Vampire bat 15

W
Whitetail deer 21

A TEMPLAR BOOK

Devised and produced by The Templar Company plc
Pippbrook Mill, London Road, Dorking,
Surrey RH4 1JE, Great Britain
Copyright © 1994 by The Templar Company plc